Contents

1 Introduction

Life in Britain today is very different from life two hundred years ago. In the past most people lived in the countryside and worked at home. Today most people live in towns and go out to work.

Britain was the first country in the world to change from a farming country to a country based on the factory system. We call this change the Industrial Revolution.

It all started with the cotton plant. This book will look at the work of ordinary people who grew this cotton and turned it into cloth and the changes that took place in their lives.

Some of the sources used in the book are shown below. Many come from the time of the event. These are called primary sources. Others were written or made after the event. These are called secondary sources.

Hansard

A summary of what MPs said in Parliament was published. After 1811, it was published by T C Hansard. In the nineteenth century MPs discussed working conditions in factories. From *Hansard* we can find out what MPs thought at the time.

Official reports

Government committees often interviewed ordinary people to find out about their lives. Michael Sadler, an MP, wanted to pass a law to limit the hours of children working in factories. He interviewed 89 cotton workers. No factory owner was interviewed by Sadler. No evidence was taken on oath.

The Government did not really accept Sadler's report and made their own enquiries. Edwin Chadwick was asked to interview both factory workers and factory owners. Many factory workers refused to talk to Chadwick.

A Hansard

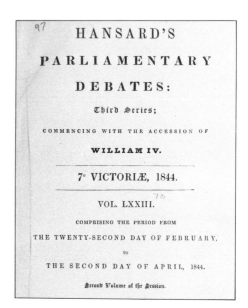

HANSARD'S PARLIAMENTARY DEBATES: Third Series; COMMENCING WITH THE ACCESSION OF WILLIAM IV. 7° VICTORIÆ, 1844. VOL. LXXIII. COMPRISING THE PERIOD FROM THE TWENTY-SECOND DAY OF FEBRUARY, TO THE SECOND DAY OF APRIL, 1844. Second Volume of the Session.

"The excessive fatigue, privation of sleep, pain in various parts of the body, and swelling of the feet, experienced by the young workers, coupled with the constant standing, the peculiar attitudes of the body, and the peculiar motion of the limbs required in the labour of the factory, together with the elevated temperature, and the impure atmosphere in which the labour is often carried on, do sometimes ultimately terminate in the production of serious, permanent, and incurable diseases."

Doctor Loudon states—

"I think it has been already proved that children have been worked a most unreasonable and cruel length of time daily, and that even adults have been expected to do a certain quantity of labour, which scarcely any human being is able to endure. As a physician, I would prefer the limitation of ten hours for all persons who earn their bread by their industry."

Doctor Hawkins says—

"I am compelled to declare my deliberate opinion, that no child should be employed in factory-labour below the age of ten, that no individual under the age of eighteen should be employed in it longer than ten hours daily."

B *A 19th century newspaper.*

The Voice of the People.

"THE GREATEST HAPPINESS TO THE GREATEST NUMBER."
"WHEN THE CONDITION OF THE LABOURER IS DEPRESSED, THE PROSPERITY OF THE OTHER CLASSES CAN REST ON NO SOLID FOUNDATION."

No. 15.—Vol. 1.   SATURDAY, APRIL 9, 1831.   Paper, Print, &c.....3d. Taxes on Knowledge, 4d. 7D. Price.

Newspapers and maps

Newspapers are very important for an historian. The larger, national newspapers tell us mostly about big events, but the local papers will contain news about a small area. But newspapers have their own version of the truth and their own point of view.

Paintings and drawings

There were no cameras two hundred years ago so we have to rely on paintings and drawings. Pictures can tell us a lot about how people lived and worked. But when you look at a picture you must think about who drew it and why it was drawn.

Sometimes artists sketched pictures to make something look more attractive than it really was. Other artists drew the same topic to make it look dreadful.

Some pictures that were drawn for novels are now used in history books. It is also important to remember that many pictures have been destroyed over time.

Oral history

People today can often give us information that we do not find in most history books. It is often the best way of finding out about ordinary people's lives. But their memories are not always reliable, and there are few people alive today who can give us information about the nineteenth century.

Other written evidence

Books written at the time can help us to understand what people thought in the past. **Autobiographies** help us get closer to how people felt. But sometimes people will leave out bits of their lives. They might also try to make their lives seem more important than they really were.

History books can be useful too. Before researching a topic, historians look at the secondary sources which have been written.

Historians may have information that was not available to people living at the time. But all historians have their own point of view. So, see what bias you can find in this book!

Questions

1 a) What is the difference between a primary and a secondary source?
b) Can you always tell whether a source is primary or secondary? Give reasons.
c) Are primary sources more reliable than secondary sources? Give reasons.

2 Look at source A. What might be the danger of relying on MPs for evidence?

3 Read the paragraph about Official Reports.
a) Whom did Sadler interview?
b) Whom did Sadler miss out?
c) Chadwick interviewed both factory owners and factory workers. Does this make him less biased? Give reasons.

4 Look at source B.
Would this paper support the factory workers or the factory owners? Give reasons.

5 Try to obtain a copy of the *Sun* and *The Guardian*. Look at the front page. What do you notice about: the size of the page; the headlines; the content?

6 What do readers of history books (including yourself) have to be wary of?

2 Working at Home

Everyone in the world today wears clothes. These clothes might be made of natural material such as wool from animals or cotton from plants. **Artificial** materials such as polyester made from oil are also worn.

Two hundred years ago in Britain most people wore clothes made from wool and sometimes cotton. There were no artificial fabrics. These materials were usually made in the homes of ordinary people. In many homes the men, women and children all worked together to make cloth. This was called the domestic system of industry.

The first step in making cloth was to clean the wool or cotton. This was called 'carding'. Cards were two flat brushes with wire bristles. Cotton was put on one brush whilst the other brush was drawn over it again and again.

The cotton was then cleaned in a tub of soapy liquid. Cleaning wool was even messier.

A *Chapman,* The Cotton Manufacture of Great Britain, *1861:*

> The next process was wet and messy for the piece had to be [well-cleaned] to remove the Grease. The liquid used was stale urine or 'weeting' as it was called. The stone floor of the living room was used for this. All the furniture was removed and the piece was spread over the floor, sprinkled with urine from a watering can and scrubbed.

Drying the material was not an easy job in small cottages. Sometimes houses caught fire when people dried it too quickly.

B *A diary which was written by someone called Rowbotham in 1788 said:*

> Fire at Isaac Hardy's, which burnt 6lbs of cotton, five pairs of stockings and set the [cot] on fire, with a child in which was much burnt. It happened through

the wife holding the candle under the cotton as it was drying.

The clean and carded cotton was next spun on a spinning wheel into yarn. Spinning wheels were first used in India and were copied in Britain in about 1300. Before the spinning wheel women used a distaff to make yarn.

C *A woman spinning with a distaff.*

D *This is an Indian spinning wheel used by women for centuries.*

The yarn was woven on to a hand-loom and later bleached. Cotton was often bleached by the sun.

E *Working at home.*

F *Bleachfields, Glasgow 1844.*

Questions

1   a) Make a list of all the clothes you are wearing today.
b) What materials are they made from?
c) Which part of the world do they come from?
d) Which of these materials existed in the eighteenth century?

2   Look at sources C and D. What advantages are there in using the spinning wheel?

3   Look at source E.
a) Which member of the family did the: carding; spinning; weaving?
b) What other jobs in the home might have to be done?

4   Look at source F.
a) How was the cotton bleached?
b) What were the problems in bleaching cloth this way?

3 Life at Home

Most textile workers worked in their own home making wool or cotton. They usually lived in the countryside in small cottages. Cottages were either made of stone or of clay and mud. Thatched roofs were common. The floor was often made of earth. Usually there was only one room on the ground floor with two bedrooms above. There might be a few small windows which could not be opened.

Cottages could be very cold in the winter. They were draughty, damp and dark. In summer they were often too hot and airless. As families were quite large these cottages were usually overcrowded. People ate, cooked, worked and slept in them.

Some people who travelled around Britain described these cottages very differently. Some saw them as sturdy and comfortable homes whilst others described them as hovels.

A *Arthur Young,* Northern Tours, *1771:*

I should not forget to remark, that the village is one of the neatest, best built ... I have ever seen, most of the houses and cottages are new built, all of them tiled, and many of brick.

B Morning Chronicle, *1849:*

I found them neat, warm and comfortable and clean ... [with] ... a common room, a scullery behind it and two more bedrooms ... The floors were stone-flagged, nicely sanded ... the furniture massive and old fashioned.

C *William Cobbett,* Rural Rides, *1830:*

Look at these **hovels**, made of mud and straw; bits of glass, or of old cast off windows, without frames, hinges, frequently, but merely stuck in the mud wall. Enter them and look at the bits of chairs or stools, the wretched boards tacked together to serve for a table; the floor of pebble, broken brick, or of bare ground; look at the thing called a bed ... the rags on the backs.

D *William Howitt,* The Rural Life of England, *1838:*

What a mighty space lies between the palace and the cottage in this country ... naked walls, bare brick, stone or mud floor ... a few wooden, or rush bottomed chairs; a deal, or old oak table; a simple fire place, with its oven beside it ... a few pots and pans.

E *Cottage as imagined by a Victorian artist, 1863.*

Some people liked working in these homes because they could stop and start work when they wished. Others had no time for relaxation.

F *Inside a cottage, 1846.*

G *A cottage built of mud and thatch.*

H *A weaver, 1820:*

I then worked in a small chamber, overlooking Luddenden Churchyard. I used to go out in the fields and woods ... at meal times, and listen to the songs of the summer birds.

I *Poem from Leeds Reference Library, about 1730:*

So thou's setting me my work
I think I'd more need mend they sark [shirt]
And me to bake and swing and blend,
And washing yup, morn, noon and neet,
And bowls to scald and milk to fleet
And barns to fetch again at neet.

Questions

1   Read sources A, B, C and D.
   a) How do these sources disagree?
   b) Why do you think these sources disagree?

2   Look at source E.
   a) What can this source show us about life at this time?
   b) How reliable is this source as evidence? Give reasons for your answer.
   c) Which piece of written evidence does this source support?

3   Look at source F.
   a) What can this source tell an historian about home life at this time?
   b) How is it different from source E?

4   Read sources H and I
   a) What does each of these writers say about working at home?
   b) Why do these sources disagree?

4 Inventions

Materials made from cotton soon became more popular than material made from wool.

A *W Radcliffe*, The Origins of Power Loom Weaving, *1828:*

> From the year 1770–1788 . . . wool had disappeared altogether and . . . linen was also nearly gone: cotton, cotton, cotton has become the almost **universal** material.

Cotton was easier to wash than wool and more comfortable to wear. The invention of new machinery made cotton cloth much cheaper.

The Flying Shuttle:

This machine was invented by John Kay in the early 1730s. It allowed one man to weave wider cloth.

The Spinning Jenny:

James Hargreaves made a simple wooden spinning machine in about 1765. Instead of spinning one thread on the spinning wheel this machine could spin many threads at once.

The Water Frame:

The water frame was a spinning machine. It was a large machine which worked by water. Richard Arkwright built a factory at Cromford in 1771 to use water frames. People now left their homes to go out to work for a wage.

The Mule:

In 1779 Samuel Crompton invented a spinning machine which was much better than the water frame. This machine made much finer thread.

The Power Loom:

In 1784 Edmund Cartwright built a weaving machine which was later worked by steam. Most of these machines were too big to fit into an ordinary cottage so factories were built to put them in.

The Cotton Gin:

Gin is short for engine. The cotton gin separated the seeds from the cotton plant. It speeded up the cleaning of cotton. One gin could clean fifty times the amount of cotton that a slave could.

The Cotton Gin

Plantation owners were very pleased with the cotton gin. English factories needed a lot of raw cotton. The gin supplied cotton quickly and cheaply. Many history books say that Eli Whitney invented this machine. As you can see from some of the sources below, some people disagree. See if you can make your mind up!

B *Eli Whitney wrote a letter to his father on 13 September 1793 which said:*

There were a number of respectable gentlemen at Mrs Green's who all agreed that if a machine could be invented that could clean cotton . . . it would be a great thing . . . I happened to be thinking on the subject and struck out a plan of a machine in my mind . . . In about ten days I made a little model.

C *D L Cohn (historian),* The Life and Times of King Cotton, *1956:*

The would-be inventor [told] his plan to Mr Miller . . . Miller urged Whitney to experiment at his expense and they agreed that any profits . . . should be shared equally . . . Phineas Miller married his wealthy employer, Mrs Green, and Whitney supplied with money, [built] a gin factory at New Haven.

D *Brawley (historian),* A Social History of the American Negro, *1921:*

Eli Whitney, a **graduate** of Yale, went to Georgia and was employed as a teacher by the widow of General Greene on her plantation. Seeing the need of some machine for the more rapid separating of the cotton seed, he [worked] until in 1793 he succeeded. The tradition . . . is that the real credit of the invention belongs to a Negro on the plantation.

E *Sheila Lewenhak (historian),* Women and Work, *1980:*

The invention that picked the seeds out 20 times as quickly as a female hand-picker, and which finally made cotton 'King' was the cotton gin. It was Mrs Catherine Littlefield Green, a general's widow, who herself ran a cotton plantation, who thought of [using wire instead of wooden teeth, the main change.] Her lodger, Eli Whitney, who actually made the machine in consultation with her claimed the **patent rights** which she was too **genteel** to claim herself. The cotton gin is known as his invention.

Questions

1   a) List all the spinning and weaving inventions.
b) Why was each of these inventions important to the growth of the cotton trade?
c) Which of the five do you think was the most important? Give reasons.
d) Why do you think cotton became cheaper?

2   Read sources B – E.
a) Who, according to each source, invented the gin?
b) List all the points on which these sources agree.
c) Why do you think these sources disagree?
d) Does this disagreement make them all useless as evidence? Give reasons.

3   Suggest reasons why Eli Whitney's letter might not tell the whole truth.

11

5 Working in a Factory

At first cotton mills were run by water and built near streams in the countryside. Most factories were spinning factories. Arkwright built the first successful cotton-spinning mill in the small village of Cromford using water from the Bonsall brook.

Others copied Arkwright's idea and factories were built in many other quiet, country villages. By 1788 there were more than 40 spinning mills in Lancashire.

Lancashire was a good place to manufacture cotton. There were many rivers which had soft water. The climate was very damp. This was important because cotton thread broke in a dry atmosphere. If you look at the map you can also see that Lancashire was near the port of Liverpool.

Steam was later used to work the machines. There was no need for factories to be built near rivers so bigger factories were built in towns. In 1786 Manchester had only one spinning mill, yet fifteen years later there were about fifty.

A *This map shows the main cotton towns of Britain:*

B *This is a picture of a factory in the country in about 1811:*

C *A factory in a town:*

Most workers in the early factories were women and children. A few men were employed as **overseers** or engineers. Most husbands and fathers stayed at home weaving.

As bigger and more powerful machines were invented, factories became larger. Every member of the family then went out to work for wages. Each person had a different job in the factory.

Children usually worked as 'scavengers' or 'piecers'. Scavengers picked up the bits of thread and cotton fluff underneath the machines. Piecers joined together the ends of broken thread.

D *David Rowlands,* Report on Factory Children's Labour, *1831:*

[The scavenger] has to take the brush and sweep under the wheels of the spinning machines.

E Morning Chronicle, *about 1850:*

The ordinary mule, used for 'fine' work, requires a spinner, two piecers, and a scavenger ... He employs his own piecers and his own scavenger.

F *A weaving factory in about 1900:*

Most of the weavers were women. Women were also **tenters**, carders, **throstle spinners** and sometimes piecers. Some women were also employed on the smaller mules.

A few men, called overseers, were employed to make sure that everyone worked hard. But most men in the factories worked as mule spinners. Mule spinners were paid **piece-rates** and employed their own helpers. They were so important that the best rooms in some pubs were marked 'Mule Spinners only'.

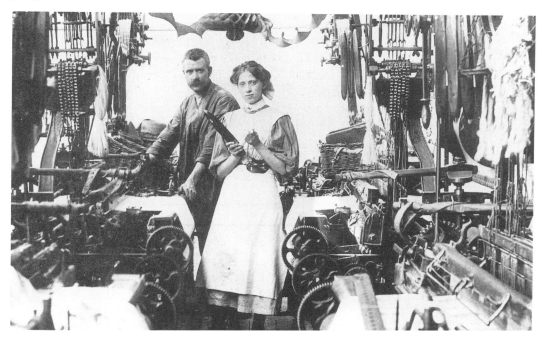

Questions

1 Look at source A. Why was being near Liverpool so important for the cotton trade?

2 Look at sources B and C.
a) What are the main differences between these two sources?
b) Why do you think these pictures are so different?
c) Pick out three things from each picture and say what they might show an historian about living near a factory.

3 Why do you think children were usually employed as a) scavengers b) piecers?

4 Look at source F.
a) Who is the man in the picture?
b) What machine is the woman working?

5 Look back to Chapter 2 to answer questions a) and b).
a) Who did the spinning at home?
b) Who did the weaving at home?
c) Who did most of the spinning in a factory?
d) Who did most of the weaving in a factory?
e) What effect do you think this change in jobs might have had on men and women?
f) Can you think of any other jobs done by men today that women used to do?

6 Pauper Apprentices

Many factory owners employed orphan children because they could not get enough adults to work for them. These were usually pauper apprentices who had been sent by **workhouses** in London to factories in the North of England. Factory owners paid a lump sum of money for them. They were supposed to teach them a trade.

Most children began working at seven years of age. They were not allowed to leave the factory until they were 21. Instead of wages, pauper apprentices were given food and clothes.

They all lived in a house provided by the factory owner. Most of them were girls because boy paupers were often apprenticed to a trade such as chimney sweeping.

A few factory owners treated their children kindly. Pauper apprentices were given a little pocket money each week and had decent clothes to wear. They lived in a clean house and were well-fed.

Other pauper apprentices were treated badly. They were dressed in rags. Many slept three or four to a bed. At times, the children were so hungry they had to eat food meant for pigs.

A former apprentice, Robert Blincoe, told his story to John Brown, a journalist, when he was thirty. Brown first published Blincoe's story in 1828 to shock people. It was reprinted in 1832 just before Parliament set up an enquiry into factory conditions.

A *This is the second edition of Blincoe's* Memoirs:

A

MEMOIR
OF

ROBERT BLINCOE,

An Orphan Boy;

SENT FROM THE WORKHOUSE OF ST. PANCRAS, LONDON,
AT SEVEN YEARS OF AGE,

TO ENDURE THE

Horrors of a Cotton-Mill,

THROUGH HIS INFANCY AND YOUTH,

WITH A MINUTE DETAIL OF HIS SUFFERINGS,

BEING

THE FIRST MEMOIR OF THE KIND PUBLISHED.

BY JOHN BROWN.

MANCHESTER:
PRINTED FOR AND PUBLISHED BY J. DOHERTY, 37, WITHY-GROVE.
1832.

B *John Brown,* A Memoir of Robert Blincoe, *1832:*

Blincoe heard the burring sound . . . and smelt the fumes of the oil . . . The moment he entered the doors, the noise [horrified] him, and the [smell] seemed [unbearable].

The [job] first [given] to him was, to pick up the loose cotton, that fell upon the floor. Apparently, nothing could be easier . . . although [he was] much terrified by the . . . noise of the machinery.
Many . . . had by this time, been more or less injured by the machinery. Some had the skin scraped off the knuckles, clean to the bone . . . others a finger crushed, a joint or two nipped off . . .

When his turn to suffer came, the fore-finger of his left hand was caught and almost before he could cry out, off was the first joint . . . he clapped the [squashed] joint, streaming with blood, to the finger, and ran off to . . . the surgeon, who . . . put the parts together again and sent him back to the mill.

To lift the apprentices up by their ears, shake them violently and then [throw] them down upon the floor with . . . fury, was one of the many inhuman sports in Litton Mill . . . Frequently has Blincoe been thus treated, till he thought his ears were torn from his head . . . Another . . . consisted in filing apprentices' teeth.

Blincoe declared that he had often been [forced],

on a cold winter's day, to work naked, except his trousers, and loaded with two half hundred-weights slung behind him, hanging one at each shoulder.
It is a fact ... that the most brutal ... have been in the habit of ... [forcing] them to eat dirty pieces of candle, to lick up tobacco spit, to open their mouths for the filthy wretches to spit into.

Many mill owners said that they treated their children well.

C *Mr Davison and Mr Hawksley, factory owners, said in 1798:*

I declare to you in the most [serious] manner, that neither my partner nor myself would conduct our business at the expense of humanity, or otherwise, than by a kind and generous [behaviour] towards those children ...

D *From a novel called* The Factory Boy *by Frances Trollope, published 1839:*

E *In their advertisements for young people Davison and Hawksley promised that boys and girls employed by them would:*

be well-clothed, lodged and boarded, they will attend church every Sabbath.

F *Almond and Lambert, owners of another mill, also said that they treated their apprentices decently. Their children:*

were kept decently clad ... were occasionally allowed a little time for play in the open air ... They were worked hard: but not hard as to distort their limbs ... Their bedding, though coarse, was clean ... they were humanely treated.

Questions

1   Look at source A.
a) What is this book about?
b) Pick out some words that show the bias of the author.

2   Read source B.
a) What can source B tell us about conditions for pauper apprentices? Mention the noise, the smell, the hours, the accidents, the beatings.
b) What is the writer trying to make you feel? Explain how you decided.

3   Read sources C, E, and F.
a) What can these sources tell us about conditions for pauper apprentices?
b) How do these sources differ from sources A and B?

4   Look at source D.
a) How are the boys in this picture dressed?
b) What do you think they might be eating?
c) Which piece of written evidence best supports this picture?

5   a) Why do these sources differ?
b) Which do you think is the most reliable and why?
c) What were the motives of each writer or artist?

7 Factory Conditions

Every factory was damp, dusty and noisy. Spinning and weaving machines were deafening. Fluff and cotton dust was everywhere. Many workers stood in their bare feet in puddles of water. Buckets in the corner of the room were sometimes used as lavatories.

Hours were long and tiring. There was a break in the middle of the day. To shorten this break some factory owners put the clock forward at the beginning of lunch-time.

A *Joseph Haberjam, a worker, told* Sadler's Committee, *1831–1833:*

> You cannot take food out of your basket or handkerchief but what is covered in dust . . . The children are frequently sick because of the dust and dirt they eat with their meal.

B *An interview with a worker by* Gregg's Committee, *1832:*

> At what time in the morning in the [busy] time, did those girls go to the mills?
>
> In the [busy] time, for about six weeks they have gone at 3 o'clock in the morning, and ended at ten, or nearly half-past at night.

C *Edwin Chadwick,* The Sanitary Condition of the Labouring Population of Great Britain, *1842:*

> The feet of the female as well as of the male workers . . . who work in the mills without their stockings, are seen [covered] with the filth of years.

D *Report from the* Central Board of HM's Commissioners in Factories, *1833:*

> I have heard it said that the minute hand used to tumble when it got to the top at dinner time: it very seldom tumbled at any other time. I have seen it drop myself . . . five minutes, so that when it was really 12 o'clock it would drop to five minutes after 12.

E *Women carding:*

F *Edwin Chadwick,* The Sanitary Condition of the Labouring Population of Great Britain, *1842:*

> . . . the factories . . . are all of them drier and warmer than the [home] of the parent; and we had proof that weakly children have been put into the better-managed factories as healthier places for them than their own homes.

G *Adapted from* Factories Inquiry, *1834:*

Work	Age and Sex of worker	Wages for 69-hour week
MULE SPINNERS		
Overlooker	Male Adults	1.50p
Spinners	Male Adults	1.27p
Piecers	Children	26p
Scavengers	Children	12p
WEAVERS		
Overlookers	Male Adults	1.30p
Weavers	Female Adults	61p

Many employers fined their workers to make sure they behaved themselves and worked hard. Workers were usually fined because they opened windows, talked or whistled. Some factory owners allowed their workers to be beaten. Fining people was thought to be kinder.

H *Fines at Strutt's Mill, Belper, 1805–1815:*

Leaving without giving notice
Idleness and looking thro' window
Stealing packthread
Breaking thermometer
[Noisy] behaviour in room
Throwing bobbins at people
Running away
Breaking a drawing Frame
Being off with a pretence of being ill, when on sending [someone] up [to] where she lives she was found washing
Setting fire to a lamp cupboard

I *Mule spinners, 1900:*

Riding on each others back
Dancing in room
Throwing bobbins at people
Neglecting their work
Having waste found on her
Putting good cotton in the dust
Leaving her machine dirty
Refusing to clean her frames
Striking T Ride on the nose
Calling through window to some soldiers
Being off drinking
Off without [permission] with soldiers
For stealing candles, oil etc
Setting fire to a lamp cupboard
Throwing water on Ann Gregory very frequently
Going off with some Militia men
Neglecting his work to talk to people
Sending for ale in the room
Tearing roller cloths wilfully
Leaving her machine dirty
Damping her cotton

Questions

1 Read sources A – D and look at source I.
a) What can these sources tell us about factory conditions?
b) What illnesses might a worker suffer from?

2 Read source F.
a) How does Chadwick describe most factories?
b) Does Chadwick's account make sources A – D useless as evidence? Give reasons.

3 Look at source G.
a) Which adult was paid the most?
b) Which adult was paid the least?
c) Why do you think women and children worked for so little?

4 Look at source H.
At Strutt's Mill, Belper, workers were fined for (a) being absent without permission, (b) stealing, (c) destroying property, (d) not working properly and (e) behaving badly. For each of these rules, give two examples of how the workers broke it, e.g. 'Riding on each others back' was behaving badly.

8 Robert Owen

Robert Owen was born in Wales in 1771. His first job was as a pupil teacher. Later he moved to Manchester and began work in a **draper's shop**. Next, Owen worked in a factory. By the time he was 29 he owned a large factory in New Lanark, near Glasgow.

A *New Lanark:*

Robert Owen was an unusual man. He believed people were naturally good. People only behaved badly because the world in which they lived was unfair. Owen wanted to change this world into a place where everyone co-operated. He also thought that women were treated unfairly and admired the women at this time who struggled for equality.

B *Adapted from* The Life of Robert Owen by Himself, *1857:*

> If people were treated, trained, educated and employed properly there would be no crime. People would also not be miserable. Everyone would be wealthy and wise.

C *Factory workers at New Lanark:*

As a factory owner, Robert Owen believed that if workers were well treated they would work harder. At New Lanark, Owen reduced hours and put up wages. He built houses, schools and community halls for his workers. Yet he still made a profit.

When Owen first arrived at New Lanark many pauper apprentices worked there. Owen refused to take any more. He only employed chidren over ten years of age who lived in the neighbourhood with their parents.

Owen began a school at New Lanark in 1816. Children started school at the age of three and stayed there until they were ten. Children could stay on at school until they were 13 if their parents could do without their wages.

Children at the school did not learn from books all the time. Instead they learnt about plants and flowers through nature trails. Pictures and maps on the wall taught them about geography and other subjects.

Exercise and fresh air were thought to be important. Dancing, singing and playing musical instruments were also encouraged.

Owen was unable to put all his ideas into practice in Britain. In 1824 he sailed to America and bought a place called New Harmony. Here there was good farming land. There were also mills, houses and community buildings.

Owen set to work to make his dream come true. Everyone was to work together and share the profits. People would all help each other and live peacefully. It would be a new world.

This idea did not work. Robert Owen allowed anyone to come to live in New Harmony and it soon became over-crowded. People argued with each other.

Leaving his son in charge, Robert Owen left America and returned to Britain. He had lost most of his money trying out this idea.

When Owen returned to England he tried to change the world another way. In 1833 he set up the Grand National Consolidated Trades Union. Both employers and workers were encouraged to join it. The GNCTU tried to improve working conditions. Many employers did not like this. They tried to make their workers sign a document promising not to join the GNCTU. As a result there were many strikes. Gradually the GNCTU ran out of money and collapsed.

Although many of Owen's ideas failed, his influence can still be seen today. Many towns in Britain still have Co-op shops. Co-op shops came from the ideas of Owen. These shops give back any profit they make to the customer. Most shops give their profits to the people who own them.

E *Even Robert Owen recognised that his ideas were advanced. On his deathbed in 1858 he said:*

I gave important truths to the world, and it was only for want of understanding that they were disregarded. I have been ahead of my time.

Questions

1 Read source B.
a) What, according to Robert Owen, caused crime and misery?
b) Do you agree or disagree with Owen? Give reasons for your answer.

2 Robert Owen put up wages and reduced hours at New Lanark yet still made a profit. Why do you think this was so?

3 Look at source D.
a) How are the girls and the boys dressed?

b) Who might be the people watching the dance?
c) Why might Owen think dancing important?
d) Look at the wall. What lesson might be taught to the pupils, using this picture?

4 Read source E.
a) What did Owen mean when he said that 'he was ahead of his time'?
b) Do you think Owen's ideas would work today? Give reasons for your answer.

9 Pictures as Evidence

The introduction to this book said that pictures, as well as writing, could be biased. The pictures on these two pages show different aspects of factory life.

These pictures show mule-spinning machines. See if you can spot the difference!

A *From a novel called* Michael Armstrong, Factory Boy *by Frances Trollope, 1840:*

B The Progress of Cotton *by J R Barfoot, a book published for the* Ladies Society for Promoting the Early Education of Negro Children, *1835–1840:*

C *From a book called* The White Slaves *by John Cobden, 1860:*

THE WHITE SLAVES OF ENGLAND.

D *From Frances Trollope's novel:*

E *A 19th century painting:*

Questions

1   Look at source A.
a) Who do you think the man in the top hat is?
b) What is he holding in his hand?
c) Who do you think the other men in the picture are?
d) Compare the clothes of the two boys in the front of this picture.

2   Look at source B.
a) What work are the women doing?
b) What work is the man doing?
c) What work is the child doing?

3   Look at source C.
a) What is A doing?
b) Suggest a reason why he might be doing this.

4   Look at sources A, B and C again and read the captions carefully.
a) What is similar in each of these pictures?
b) What is different about each of these pictures?
c) What impression did each artist want to give about factory life?
d) How reliable is each of these sources?
e) What are the disadvantages of using novels as evidence?
f) How useful are these sources to an historian? Give reasons for your answer.

5   Look at source D. In what way does the artist show factory life as unpleasant? (Think about how the people are dressed, how they are standing, the time of year.)

6   Look at source E.
a) Do the workers look well dressed or badly dressed? Explain your answer.
b) In what other way is this source different from Source D?
c) Why are two sources showing the same picture so different?

21

10 Other Cotton Workers

It was too cold to grow cotton in Britain. At first cotton came from India. When Europeans were still wearing animal skins, the people of India were wearing clothes of fine cotton. Indian cotton was the best for thousands of years. One traveller said that it 'was so fine that you can hardly feel it in your hand'.

Much later, slaves working in America grew most of the cotton for Britain. They were bought in Africa and taken in ships called 'slavers' to America. If they survived the journey across the Atlantic they were sold and forced to work on sugar, tobacco or cotton **plantations**.

Cotton grown in America was brought to Britain on the slave ships and made into cloth. These slavers then carried the cloth, along with beads, chains, alcohol and other goods to Africa to exchange for slaves. This was known as the 'Slave Triangle'.

A *The Slave Triangle:*

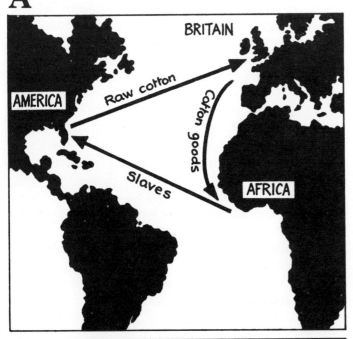

Many large plantations had managers called 'overseers' who had to look after the plantation.

The owner was often absent. Beneath this overseer were one or more slave drivers who had to keep order amongst the field slaves.

Cotton was planted at the end of March and picked in August. Men, women and children all worked on the cotton plantation. There were different jobs to do throughout the year.

Slaves worked in the fields from the age of ten. Everyone worked hard from early in the morning until after dark. Each morning before daylight the slaves were woken by the sound of a horn blown by the overseer.

B *J H Ingrahams,* Southwest by a Yankee, *1860:*

The [workers] are required to be in the cotton fields as soon as it is light in the morning. With the exception of fifteen minutes which is given them at noon to swallow their allowance of cold bacon, they are not [allowed] to be a moment idle until it is too dark to see. When the moon is full, they often times **labor** til the middle of the night.

C *Frederick Law Olmsted,* A Journey in the Back Country, *1860:*

The plowing, both with single and double mule teams, was generally [done] by women, and very well [done] too.

D *Solomon Northrup,* Twelve Years a Slave, *1853:*

A girl usually drops the seed, which she carries in a bag hung around her neck. Behind her comes a mule and harrow, covering up the seed ... this is done in the months of March and April.

E *Frederick Law Olmsted,* A Journey in the Back Country, *1860:*

In August begins the cotton picking season. At this time each slave is [given] a sack and a large basket. When the sack is filled, it is emptied into the basket and trodden down.

F *J H Ingrahams,* Southwest by a Yankee, *1860:*

... each hand is [given] a large basket, and two coarse cotton bags about the size of a pillow case, with a strong strap to suspend them from the neck or shoulders. The basket is left at the end of a row, and both bags taken along ... As soon as the second is full, he returns to the basket, taking the other bag as he passes it, and emptying both into the basket, treading it down well.

G *Picking the cotton:*

H *Taking the cotton to be weighed:*

I *Solomon Northrup,* Twelve Years a Slave, *1853:*

The day's work over in the field the baskets are ... carried to the gin house where the cotton is weighed. No matter how ... weary he may be ... no matter how much he longs for sleep and rest – a slave ... approaches the gin house with his basket of cotton ... with fear. If it falls short of weight ... he knows that he must suffer ...

Questions

1   Look at source A.
   a) What goods were exchanged for slaves?
   b) How important was the slave trade to cotton?

2   Read source B.
   a) What hours were worked by slaves?
   b) A Yankee was a northern white American. Is this source reliable? Give reasons.

3   Read sources E and F and look at source G.
   a) What happened to A when it was full?
   b) What happened to B?

4   Read source I and look at source H.
   a) How are the slaves carrying the baskets of cotton?
   b) These slaves are all walking erectly. How does the picture compare to the written source?
   c) How valuable are both these sources to an historian?

5   You are a slave, returning from a day's work in the fields. Describe what you might feel. Choose some of the following words to help you: tired; exhausted; relieved; happy; sleepy; over-worked.

11 Plantation Life

A slave on a plantation was owned by another person, just as a video, a car, a house or even a computer is owned. A slave was a piece of property that could be bought or sold.

Slaves had no rights at all. They could not own their own home or buy anything. Slaves needed permission to have a drink of alcohol, or to get married. Many were not allowed to learn to read or write. If slaves disobeyed any of these laws they were severely punished.

A *These were the rules of the State of Alabama in 1852. They show how slaves could be punished if they broke the law:*

1009 If any slave go upon the plantation . . . without permission in writing from his master or overseer . . . ten lashes on his bare back.

1012 No slave can keep or carry a gun, powder, shot, club, or other weapon . . . [then the] slave receive thirty-nine lashes on his bare back.

1022 Any slave who preaches . . . without a license . . . be punished with thirty-nine lashes, and for the second, with fifty lashes.

B *Ann Clark, an ex-slave aged 112, 1937:*

My poppa was strong. He never had a lick in his life. He helped the master, but one day the master says 'Si, you got to have a whipping' and my poppa says 'I never had a whipping and you can't whip me.' And the master said 'But I can kill you' and he shot my poppa down.

Many rebelled against this slavery. Some slaves cut off their toes and hands so that they could not work. Mothers killed their babies to prevent them becoming slaves.

Other slaves pretended to be lame, sick, blind or stupid to avoid work. Slave masters were sometimes poisoned by slaves putting ground glass or arsenic in their food.

C *Runaway slaves:*

Very many slaves ran away. One North Carolina woman ran away sixteen times. It was against the law to help runaway slaves yet many people put themselves at risk to help them.

D *One slave in the nineteenth century told of her experience in helping runaways:*

I heard a rap – bump bump on my door. I answered. Then someone whispered 'Hush, don't say nothing, but let me in.' I let her in . . . that woman was all out of breath and begging 'Can I stay here tonight?'

I told her she could, so the woman done sleep right there behind me in my bed all night. I knew she had run away, and I was gonna do my part to help her along.

I . . . heard the horses and talking in the woods. Dogs barking. I peeped out the window and saw white folks go by. I didn't move. I was so scared they was gonna come in the cabin and search for the poor woman. Next morning she stole out from there and I never seen her no more.

An organisation called the 'Underground Railroad' helped many slaves to escape. The

Underground Railroad was not really a railway. It was a name given by slaves to hiding places in barns, cellars, woodsheds, caves and homes.

One ex-slave called Harriet Tubman risked her life to help about 300 slaves escape. She was one of the most famous 'conductors' on the railroad. At one time a reward of 40,000 dollars was offered for her capture.

Harriet Tubman

Other slaves burnt down plantations. On 21 April 1831, Nat Turner, a black preacher, led a revolt against plantation owners. Although Nat Turner was executed on 11 November 1831, many other slaves followed his example. Insurance companies refused to insure some plantations because they were burnt down so many times.

Nat Turner

A few Members of Parliament spoke out against slavery. William Wilberforce, a popular MP and a factory owner, became one of the leaders of a group in England which wanted to get rid of slavery. It took them twenty years to stop the slave trade. They succeeded in 1807.

However, it was still legal to own slaves. Not until 1833 was slavery abolished in the British Empire. Even then planters received £20 million to pay them for their lost slaves.

Although America banned the slave trade in the same year as Britain, slavery continued. Eventually, after a bitter **civil war** between the North and South, slavery ended in 1865.

Questions

1   Read through source A.
   a) How were slaves punished?
   b) Why were slaves punished?
   c) Why might slave owners fear preachers?

2   a) List all the ways slaves rebelled against slavery.
   b) Which of these do you think was the most dangerous? Give reasons for your answer.

   c) Which of these do you think was the hardest to do? Give reasons for your answer.

3   Read source D and look at source C. What do these sources tell you about the difficulties faced by runaway slaves?

4   Draw a poster persuading people to put an end to slavery.

25

12 Luddism

As you know from Chapter 4 (pages 10–11) there were many new inventions at this time. This meant that many people lost their job. Some people tried to turn the clock back and destroyed the new machines. They hoped to return to their old way of life.

There were riots against John Kay's Flying Shuttle. Richard Arkwright's factory at Birkacre near Chorley was burnt down. Only 50 invalids guarded this factory so it was probably easy to attack. Arkwright did not rebuild this mill but made sure that his other factory at Cromford was protected with cannons and guns.

Another time some women broke open James Hargreaves' house and destroyed his Jenny. Workers also attacked the inventions of Edmund Cartwright.

There is no evidence that Crompton's Mule was ever attacked. This may have been because Crompton had sold his idea to local factory owners early on. It may have been because mule spinners were highly paid workers.

Some of the people who destroyed these machines were called 'Luddites'. They were named after a man called Ned Ludd, who was supposed to live in Sherwood Forest. Ned Ludd was said to be in charge of these riots.

At first those found guilty of Luddism were put in prison. Later the Government passed a law which made Luddism a capital offence. This meant that people could be hung for breaking machines. A young boy of sixteen was once put to death for acting as sentry while his brothers burnt down a factory.

A *A pamphlet called* Thoughts on the Use of Machines in the Cotton Industry, *1780, shows the dangers faced by many inventors:*

Upon the invention of the flying shuttle by Mr John Kay of Bury . . . all the country was in uproar. His life was threatened, and was I believe in the [greatest] danger. He escaped with difficulty . . . , sewed up in a cotton bag; and went to France.

B *Some of the people who destroyed Arkwright's factory were caught, tried and convicted. From the* Quarter Sessions Orders *of 1780:*

Mary Leicester . . . Tried and Convicted at this Session . . . with several other persons to the number of Twenty and more at Birkacre within Chorley . . . entered the Mill . . . Unlawfully, Riotously and attacked and Broke, Burned and Destroyed twenty engines . . . called Spinning Engines . . . the property of Richard Arkwright . . . this court . . . Commit her . . . to his Majesty's gaol . . . for the term of twelve months.

C *Weaving machines were also destroyed in another outburst of Luddism. The* Leeds Intelligencer, *1 January 1812, reported that:*

. . . twelve men and two women were put [on trial] for setting fire to the weaving mill, warehouse and loom shop of Thomas Duncuft of Westhoughton. Their trial lasted until eight at night, when the jury retired for upwards of an hour, and brought in a verdict of Guilty against Abraham Charlston aged 16, Job Fitcher aged 34, James Smith 31 and [let off] John Bronilow, William Kay, John Shuttleworth, John Charlton, Mary Cannon, Mary Molyneux, Lydia Molyneux, Samuel Radcliffe, Robert Windward and Ada Bullough.

D *Many unemployed people could not afford to buy food. Some rioted in the street and stole food. Others forced shopkeepers to lower their prices. On Saturday 6 June 1812, the* Leeds Mercury *reported what a judge said to* **defendants** *at the end of a trial:*

. . . there to be hung by your neck until you are dead and may the Lord have mercy upon your souls . . . You, Hannah Smith, have been guilty of a robbery on the highway of a large quantity of butter . . . You have also been convicted of stealing a quantity of potatoes. This circumstance seems to prove that you were one of the most determined enemies to good order, and that . . . [your] sex is not entitled to any **mitigation** of punishment.

E One Member of Parliament, called Lord Byron, was a poet. He wrote this about the Luddites:

As the Liberty lads over the sea
Bought their freedom, and cheaply with blood
So we, boys we
Will die fighting, or live free
And down with all kings but King Ludd

F Luddites in action:

G A Luddite dressed as a woman:

Questions

1 Look at source G.
a) How is the man dressed?
b) Why do you think he might be dressed this way?
c) What has happened to the building in the background?
d) What building would it be?

2 What does the writer in source E think about the Luddites? Explain how you decided.

3 Write out source B using words which are more sympathetic to the Luddites, e.g. brave.

4 Read through source A. What problems might John Kay have had in escaping to France?

5 Read through the fourth paragraph on page 26 again.
a) What does the author give as the possible reasons for Crompton's Mule not being attacked?
b) Which do you think is the most likely explanation? Give reasons for your answer.

6 Look at source F.
a) What are the women doing in this picture?
b) How does it contrast with the other sources you have read?
c) Which do you consider to be the most reliable, the written or the visual evidence? Give reasons.

13 Reform

Laws were passed by Parliament to improve conditions in the factories.

1802   This Act applied only to water mills. Pauper apprentices were not allowed to work more than 12 hours a day. They were to be taught reading, writing and arithmetic. Factory owners were fined £5 if they broke the law.

1819   This Act applied only to cotton factories. No child under nine years of age was allowed to work. No evidence of a child's age was needed.

1833   This Act applied to most textile factories. No child under nine years of age was allowed to work. Children between nine and 13 years of age were not allowed to work more than nine hours a day. No night work allowed for anyone under the age of 18. Children working in the factory had to go to school for two hours a day. Four inspectors were appointed to make sure this law was obeyed.

1844   This Act applied to most textile factories. Women were not allowed to work for more than 12 hours a day. Children between the ages of eight and 13 were not allowed to work more than six and a half hours a day.

1847   This Act applied to most textile factories. Women and children between the ages of 13 and 16 were not allowed to work more than ten hours a day. They were not allowed to work more than 58 hours in any week. People called this the *Ten Hours Act*. A survey of 1849 showed that 70 per cent of men and only 55 per cent of women supported it.

1850   This Act applied to most textile factories. The working day to be from 6am – 6pm only. Hours were increased to ten and a half hours a day because of pressure from factory owners.

Many important people, including Members of Parliament, spoke out against factory work.

A   *Richard Oastler wrote this letter to the editor of the Agricultural and Industrial Magazine in 1835:*

Go with me to Manchester if you will, and, at 'leaving off time'– take your stand by a large gin temple;...and see the poor overworked ...'factory girl' of nine years old...all in rags and tatters; see her slur past you, to the door of the gin temple– enter with her, and you will hear her ask for a ha'porth of gin, to help her to walk home;... this is the way thousands of... females are made into 'drunkards', let England blush. And, oh, ye sincere haters of 'drunkenness' do help me to save these poor...female children.

B   *Lord Ashley, later called Lord Shaftesbury, was a rich landowner and a Member of Parliament. He supported Richard Oastler and tried to change the law. This was part of a speech that Ashley made to Parliament in support of factory reform:*

Everything runs to waste; the house and children are deserted; the wife can do nothing for her husband and family; she can neither cook, wash, repair clothes, or take charge of the infants . . . Dirt, discomfort, ignorance, recklessness, are the portion of such households.

Females . . . are forming various clubs . . . and gradually [gaining] all those privileges . . . of the male sex. These female clubs are thus described: Fifty or sixty females, married and single, form themselves into clubs . . . for protection, but in fact, they meet together, to drink, sing, and smoke, they use, it is stated, the lowest, most brutal, and most disgusting language imaginable . . .

A man came into one of these club-rooms, with a child in his arms; Come, lass, said he, addressing one of the women, come home, for I cannot keep this [child] quiet, and the other I have left crying at home.

As a result of reform in the cotton factories, there was also a campaign to stop women and children working in the mines. In 1842 a law was passed banning women and children under ten from working underground. Lord Ashley was involved in this too. Yet women continued working at the pit top unloading and sorting the coal. Interestingly, in 1842 businesses were doing very badly.

You can see what different people said about factory reform in the cartoons on this page. The pictures do not match the bubbles. You will be asked to do this yourself later on!

1. I BELIEVE THAT CHILDREN ARE BETTER OFF IN THE FACTORY THAN ON THE STREETS

A. FEMALE FACTORY WORKER

B. LOCAL DOCTOR

2. I PREFER TO WORK LONGER HOURS FOR MORE MONEY THAN WORK SHORTER HOURS FOR LESS MONEY

3. IF WE ARE STOPPED FROM WORKING IN A FACTORY WE WILL STARVE

C. FACTORY OWNER

5. ALL ENGLAND'S GREATNESS DEPENDS ON 30,000 LITTLE GIRLS IN LANCASHIRE. IF THESE LITTLE GIRLS WORK FOR TWO HOURS LESS A DAY IT WILL RUIN THE COUNTRY

E. CHILD FACTORY WORKER

4. IT WILL TAKE AWAY THE FREEDOM OF THE MILL OWNER

D. MEMBER OF PARLIAMENT

Questions

1 Read through the Factory Acts.
a) How did the reformers make sure the Acts were obeyed?
b) Do you think factory owners took much notice of:
   i) the law of 1802
   ii) the law of 1833?
Give reasons for your answer.
c) How did the 1850 Act make conditions worse?

2 Read source A.
a) Do you think Oastler supported factory reform? Give reasons.
b) What words does Oastler use to build up sympathy for the factory girl?

3 Read source B.
a) Give three reasons why Lord Ashley supported factory reform.
b) Choose another history book. What does this book say about Lord Ashley's factory reform?
c) In what way does it agree or disagree with the chapter you have just read?

4 a) Look at the cartoon strip. Match up the people in the strip with the speech bubbles, e.g. No. 1 matches up with B.
b) Pick one of the statements with which you disagree. How would you persuade the person to change his or her mind?

14 Factory Life and Slavery

Many people campaigned against both slavery and factory conditions in the nineteenth century. It was very common to compare factory workers with slaves. This may have been because the anti-slave campaign had a lot of support at this time.

A *Richard Oastler was amongst the first to make this comparison. Richard Oastler was a* **Tory** *who managed large estates near Leeds and Huddersfield. He knew nothing about factories until his friend John Wood told him about them. John Wood was the owner of a large spinning factory in Bradford. Oastler wrote this letter to the* Leeds Mercury *in 1830:*

TO THE EDITOR OF THE LEEDS MERCURY

GENTLEMEN

The fact is true . . . Thousands of . . . both males and females . . . are at this very moment existing in a state of slavery, more horrid than are the victims of that hellish system 'colonial slavery'.

Thousands of little children, both male and female, but principally female, from seven to fourteen years of age, [work] from six o'clock in the morning to seven in the evening, with only . . . thirty minutes allowed for eating and **recreation** . . .

Ye live in the boasted land of freedom, and [are sorry] that ye are slaves, and slaves without the only comfort which the negro has. He knows it is his . . . master's interest that he should live, be strong and healthy. Not so with you . . . HIRED – not sold – as slaves and daily forced to hear that they are free . . .

The blacks may be fairly compared to beasts of burden, kept for their master's use; the whites, to those which others keep and let for hire.

Oastler's letter was good publicity. It helped people who were trying to improve working conditions. As a result of Oastler's letter, factory children were often known as 'white slaves'.

B *Oastler (below) compared factory workers with slaves on many occasions. He gave this evidence to a Factory Committee in 1831–32:*

I was in the company of a West Indian slave master . . . the slave owner said 'Well, I have always thought myself disgraced by being the owner of black slaves, but we never, in the West Indies thought it was possible for any human being to be so cruel as to require a child of nine years to work a 12 and a half hour day.

Oastler's ideas were also used by others. Michael Sadler, who was one of the leaders of factory reform, said this to the House of Commons in the 1830s:

'the females of this country . . . are beaten upon the face, arms and bosom, beaten . . . as you term it, like slaves.'

Questions

1 Read source A. List the ways in which Oastler compares factory workers to slaves.

2 Read source B.
a) Why does the slave owner believe the factory system to be worse?
b) How reliable is this as evidence? Explain your answer.

3 Look carefully at source C and read the captions.
a) What does B say about slavery?
b) How does the artist show family A?
c) How does the artist show family C?
d) Which family, according to the artist, has a worse life?

4 Compare the life of a factory worker with that of a slave. Draw the chart opposite in your book to help you. Fill in the blank spaces. Look back to some of the previous chapters for information.

	Slave	Factory worker
Hours		
Wages		
Work		
Conditions (overseers, punishments etc)		
Freedom		
Resistance		
Reform		

5 Factory workers were compared with slaves yet no one compared slaves with factory workers. Why do you think this was?

15 Housing Conditions

A *Factory workers' housing at Darley Abbey, Derbyshire:*

At first factory owners built good houses for their workers. They needed to persuade people to come to work there. One factory owner, Mr Strutt, built solid, brick houses and charged between 5 and 15p rent. These houses were often white-washed and had their chimneys swept regularly.

At Darley Abbey in Derbyshire the houses were kept looking clean and pleasant by a team of painters. **Commuters** working in city areas live in these cottages today. Many of these houses had gardens where families could grow their own fruit and vegetables.

B *An advertisement to persuade people to work in Darley Mill in about 1790:*

DARLEY COTTON MILL — WANTED — FAMILIES particularly women and children to work at the said mill. They may be provided with comfortable houses and every necessary convenience either at Darley or Allestry; particularly a milking-cow to each family.

When factories moved to places like Manchester they soon made these towns smoky and dirty. Richer people lived on the outside away from the factory whilst the working class lived very close to the mill. Working-class houses were not so attractive as those built in the countryside.

These houses were built in a similar way. Most were cramped. Each house was about 3.5 metres wide and 3.6 metres long. There was only one room to each floor. A staircase was built in the middle of each room leading to the next floor. There was no back garden.

C *Many of these houses were built back-to-back:*

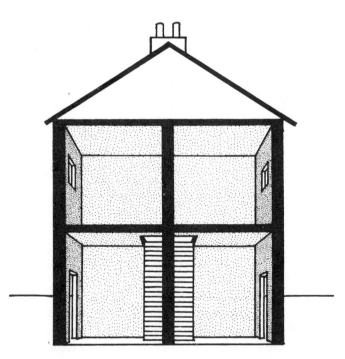

Some houses were more comfortable inside than others as the following sources show.

D *P Gaskell,* Manufacturing Population of England, *1833:*

Filthy, unfurnished ... what little furniture is found in them is of the rudest and most common sort, and very often in fragments – one or two rush-bottomed chairs, a deal table, a few stools, broken [pottery], such as dishes, tea-cups etc., one or more tin kettles and cans, a few knives and forks, a piece of broken iron, serving as a poker ... a bedstead or not ... blankets and sheets in the strict meaning of the words unknown – their place often being made up of sacking ... or a bundle of straw.

E Morning Chronicle, *about 1850:*

I visited several of the better-class houses in Hulme ... The room was about three metres by two metres, and hung with a paper of cheap quality and ordinary pattern. In at least two of the corners were cupboards of hard wood, painted mahogany fashion, and containing plates, teacups, saucers, etc.

Upon the chimney piece was [placed] a set of old-fashioned glass and china ornaments. There was one framed print hanging from the wall ... there were two tables in the apartment ... on the window ledge were two or three flower pots ... the floor was carpetless.

F *Thornton Court, Manchester, 1862:*

Questions

1 Look at source A.
a) How many rooms do you think these houses have?
b) Do you think these homes were well heated? Give reasons.
c) Is this a primary or a secondary source? Give reasons for your answer.

2 Look at source C.
a) How many rooms do you think this house has?
b) Compare this picture to source A. Why do you think these houses are so different?

3 Measure your classroom. Is it larger or smaller than the size of the average back-to-back?

4 Read sources D and E.
a) What does source D tell you about the furniture of a factory worker?
b) What does source E tell you about the furniture of a factory worker?
c) How do these sources differ?
d) Why do these sources differ?

5 Look at source F. Which pieces of evidence best support this source? Give reasons for your answer.

16 A Housing Survey

Perhaps the worst type of accommodation for factory workers was a cellar. About 15 000 very poor people lived in cellars in Manchester in the 1840s. They were damp, cheerless and dark. Very little fresh air came into these cellars.

One doctor from Liverpool said that sometimes the cellars were so wet that the people living there took the door off its hinges and laid it on the floor on top of bricks. It was difficult to keep these damp floors clean, especially since all rubbish had to be carried upstairs to the street.

A *Robert Baker, a surgeon, said this about Leeds in 1842:*

I have been in one of these damp cellars, without the slightest drainage, every drop of wet and every [piece] of dirt and filth having to be carried up into the streets; . . . beds overlaid with sacks for five persons; scarcely anything in the room else to sit on, but a stool or a few bricks; the floor, in many places absolutely wet; a pig in the corner also.

B *Another doctor reported similar conditions in Liverpool in 1845:*

I visited a poor woman in distress, the wife of a labouring man: . . . herself and infant were lying on straw in a [cellar] . . . there was no light or ventilation in it and the air was dreadful. I had to walk on bricks across the floor to reach her bedside, as the floor itself was flooded with **stagnant** water.

In 1832 J P Kay, a local doctor, did a housing survey of Manchester. He published his results in a book called *The Physical and Moral Condition of the Working Classes employed in the Cotton Manufacture in Manchester.*

Kay found that very many streets had piles of rubbish and human refuse in them. A lot of houses needed to be decorated and repaired.

C *Adapted from the results of Dr J P Kay's survey:*

District	No. of houses inspected.	No. of houses reported as requiring whitewashing	No. of houses reported as requiring repair.	No. of houses damp.	No. of houses reported as ill ventilated.	No. of houses wanting lavatories.	No. of streets containing human refuse and other rubbish.
1	850	399	128	177	70	326	64
2	2489	898	282	497	109	755	92
3	213	145	104	61	52	96	28
4	650	279	106	134	69	250	52
5	413	176	82	101	11	66	12
6	12	3	5			5	2
7	343	76	59	86	21	79	17
8	132	35	30	48	22	20	7
9	128	34	32	39	19	25	20
10	370	195	53	54	2	232	23
11							
12	113	33	23	24	16	52	4
13	757	218	44	146	54	177	23
14	481	74	13	68	7	138	8
Total	6951	2565	960	1435	452	2221	352

D *Inside a cellar:*

E *Some of the questions asked in Dr J P Kay's survey:*

INQUIRIES CONCERNING THE STATE OF HOUSES.

District. No.

Name of Street, Court, &c.   No No.   Name of Street, Court, &c.   No No.

1. Is the House in good Repair? . . . .

2. Is it clean? . . . .

3. Does it require White-washing? . . . .

4. Are the rooms well ventilated? . . . .

5. Is the house damp, or dry? . . . .

6. Are the cellars inhabited? . . . .

7. Are these inhabited cellars damp or ever flooded? . . . .

8. What number of families or lodgers does the house contain? . . . .

9. What is the state of the beds, closets, and furniture? . . . .

10. Is a private privy attached to the house?

11. Will the tenants assist in cleansing the streets and houses? . . . .

12. Are the tenants generally healthy or not?

13. What is their occupation? . . . .

14. Remarks concerning food, clothing, and fuel.

15. Habits of life.

16. General Observations.

F *A modern artist's view of a Manchester street in the 1840s:*

INQUIRIES CONCERNING THE STATE OF STREETS, COURTS, ALLEYS, &c.

District.   No.   *Inspectors.*

                    Name   Name   Name

Names of Streets, Courts, Alleys, &c.

Is the street, court, or alley narrow, and is it ill ventilated? . . . .

Is it paved or not? . . . .

Does it contain heaps of refuse, pools of stagnant fluid, or deep ruts? . . . .

Are the public and private privies well situated, and properly attended to? . . . .

Is the street, court, or alley, near a canal, river, brook, or marshy land? . . . .

General Observations . . . .

Questions

1   Read sources A and B and look at sources D and F.
a) Answer at least five of Kay's questions, basing your ideas on these sources.
b) What questions can't you answer? Why is this?
c) Where could you find the information to answer these questions?

2   Pick a house near where you live or where you go to school. See how many of Kay's questions you can answer about it.

3   What changes have taken place since Kay wrote the list of questions?

4   Look at the final results of Kay's survey in Source C. What general impression do you get about Manchester from Kay's survey?

35

17 Keeping Clean and Healthy

Today we take it for granted that most people in the western world have an inside lavatory. Most people in the nineteenth century did not have a lavatory inside the home. They used earth closets instead.

These earth closets were supposed to be emptied regularly by 'night-soil' workers. Their contents were sold to farmers as fertiliser. Unfortunately earth closets were not emptied frequently so the contents often overflowed.

Many families shared a lavatory. In two streets in one factory town there were thirty-three lavatories for about 7000 people. You can imagine what state these were in with so many people using them. The smell must have been unbearable.

Some houses had no lavatory at all. In three streets in Colne in the mid-1840s, 500 families did not have a lavatory. Most of the sewage and rubbish from all these houses was either left on the street, thrown on dung heaps or into a nearby river.

A *Edwin Chadwick,* The Sanitary Condition of the Labouring Population of Great Britain, *1842:*

In many of these places are to be seen [lavatories] in the most disgusting state of filth, open **cesspools**, [blocked] drains, ditches full of stagnant water, dunghills, pigsties etc.

Today we are used to turning on our tap to obtain fresh water. We pay a standard charge to our local authority for this each year. In many British towns in the nineteenth century, private water companies supplied water mainly to the richer houses. By our standard this service seems very limited.

So even when water was available it was not always suitable for drinking. In any case many working-class families were not at home during the period when the water was turned on. Storing water was often very difficult.

B Morning Chronicle, *about 1850:*

Generally a landlord of a set of houses sinks one or more wells, covering them of course with pumps, for the use of the tenants. The right to draw water from these sources is purchased by the neighbours at the rate from 2½ to 5p per quarter. Sometimes they come as far as half a kilometre to a favourite pump, or have the water carried home to them, paying ½p for every 14 litres.

C *Edwin Chadwick,* The Sanitary Condition of the Labouring Population of Great Britain, *1842:*

There are [many] pumps and a plentiful supply of water ... but ... the rain water is frequently like ink. The Irwell and Medlock rivers run through the town of Manchester; but being [full of] all kinds of filth and refuse, the water is too impure for general use.

D *Liverpool housing, 1906:*

E *'The water that John drinks' from* Punch, *1849:*

THIS is the water that JOHN drinks.

This is the Thames with its cento of stink,
That supplies the water that JOHN drinks.

These are the fish that float in the ink-
-y stream of the Thames with its cento of stink,
That supplies the water that JOHN drinks

This is the sewer, from cesspool and sink,
That feeds the fish that float in the ink-
-y stream of the Thames with its cento of stink,
That supplies the water that JOHN drinks.

Some towns only had rainwater barrels. At Darlington the water in one rainwater barrel was so awful that it was drained – at the bottom they found the body of a baby which had been there for months. Not surprisingly, diseases such as cholera spread very quickly. The death rate was much higher in over-crowded towns than in country areas.

Questions

1   Look at source D.
a) How many houses do you think might use this pump?
b) Do you think these houses had flush lavatories? Give reasons for your answer.

2   Read source E.
a) List all the reasons why John's water was thought to be impure.
b) Write another line of verse to continue this story. Include a drawing if you wish.

3   a) How much water do you think you use each day: for drinking; for washing; for cooking?
b) If you relied on a well for your water how many trips a day would you have to make?

4   Look at the following table which has been adapted from Chadwick's report of 1842:

Average age of death	Manchester	Rutland
Professional families	38	52
Trade families (such as farmers and shopkeepers)	20	41
Working families (labourers)	17	38

a) Who lived the longest?
b) Who died the youngest?
c) From the knowledge you have gained in this chapter, give as many reasons as you can why the death rate varied so much.

18 Cholera

Today AIDS is a shock disease. The shock diseases of the nineteenth century were typhus, typhoid and above all, cholera.

Within a few hours of catching cholera people could be dead. Usually they died within a few days. First of all they had a violent stomach ache. Next they were sick and had diarrhoea. Then they collapsed and their body went deathly cold. Lastly their pulses became weak and their skin turned a shade of blue. Then they probably died. About 40–60 per cent of victims died.

Many doctors at the time believed people caught cholera because the air was bad. Others felt that it was God's punishment for people's sins. Most agreed that cholera occurred in dirty conditions.

In fact cholera was caught from drinking water or eating food with the cholera germ in it. This germ could last up to five days in meat, fourteen days in water and sixteen days in apples. Cholera usually spread because water was infected by the **excreta** of cholera victims.

B *Chadwick,* The Sanitary Condition of the Labouring Population of Great Britain, *1842:*

In the year 1836–7 I attended a family of 13, twelve of whom had typhus fever, without a bed in the cellar, without straw or timber shavings ... They lay on the floor, and so crowded, that I could scarcely pass between them.

In another house I attended 14 patients; there were only two beds in the house. All the patients, as lodgers, lay on the boards, and during their illness, never had their clothes off ...

... it will be seen that in the township of Manchester, a population of nearly 80 000, one twenty-eighth are swept away annually, whilst, in a favoured **suburban** district, no more than one sixty-third die.

A *London family, 1863:*

C *Sketch of a girl who died of cholera*

F *Southwark in about 1860:*

D How to Avoid the Cholera *by Dr Challice of Bermondsey:*

2. Keep the whole of the body clean; do not spare soap and water . . . Cholera is fond of filth.
3. Live plainly . . . Go early to bed . . . Drunkenness and late hours are great friends of the Cholera.
4. Sleep as few in the same room, or in the same bed, as possible.
5. Early in the morning, remove all dirty or offensive matters, open your windows and doors, turn down the bed-clothes, to let the fresh air pass over them.
8. EAT ONLY OF GOOD FOOD
9. Clean out, and thoroughly wash, your water-butts or cisterns; boil the water before you drink it or give it to your children. Impure water is the cause of many diseases.
17. . . . Then, in case of sudden attack before a doctor can be fetched, apply a [cloth soaked in] vinegar and mustard over the whole belly, as long as it can be borne . . . and let the arms, feet and legs be constantly rubbed with flannels dipped in hot vinegar . . . this . . . may save many a life.

E *Parliamentary Papers 1849,* Report of the General Board of Health on Cholera:

The chief . . . causes of . . . Cholera, are damp, moisture, filth, animal and vegetable matters in a state of [decay] . . . The attacks of Cholera are . . . found to be most frequent . . . wherever there are large collections of refuse, particularly amidst human dwellings . . .

Householders of all classes should be warned, that their first means of safety lies in the removal of dung-heaps and solid and liquid filth of every description from beneath or about their houses.

Questions

1   Look at source A and read source B.
    a) In what way are these sources similar?
    b) How easy would it be for the family in Source A to become infected with cholera? Give reasons for your answer.

2   Read source B. Why might more people die of cholera in the inner city than in the country?

3   Read source D.
    a) Which part of Dr Challice's advice do you think is the most sensible?
    b) Which part of this advice do you think would be the least useful?
    c) Which of his ideas would it have been difficult for the poor to use? Give reasons.

4   Look at source F. Would cholera spread quickly in this street? Give reasons for your answer.

19 Cleaning and Cooking

Housework was a hard job for most people. Without gas or electric cookers, vacuum cleaners, washing-machines and even running water, housework was never-ending. It was usually the job of a woman to make sure the housework was done.

Most women had two jobs. All week they worked at the factory and at the weekend did all their cleaning, cooking and shopping.

A *Wash-day:*

B *Ellen Barlee wrote this in her book* Visit to Lancashire *December 1862:*

They only have this day to clean their houses, provide for the week, bake for the week, bake for the family, mend clothes, besides doing any washing that is not put out, and attend the market to [buy] the Sunday's dinner . . . then there is also washing children . . . so that the poor mother seldom gets a rest.

Many working-class people did not have an oven and had to rely on an open fire to cook their food. Most people ate potatoes and bread, drunk with tea or coffee. Men usually drank beer instead. Milk was not drunk very often. Large families in Manchester sometimes bought thirty loaves of bread a week.

C *Mr Cowell,* Lancashire District Factory Commission *1833:*

Breakfast is generally porridge, bread and milk, lined with flour or oatmeal. On Sunday, a cup of tea, bread and butter.

Dinner on week days, potatoes and bacon, and bread, which is generally white. On a Sunday, a little flesh meat: no butter egg or pudding.

Tea time – every day, tea, and bread and butter.

Supper – oatmeal porridge and milk, sometimes potatoes and milk Sunday, sometimes a little bread and cheese for supper.

D *Dr Edward Smith,* Practical Dietary for Families, Schools and the Labouring Classes, *1864:*

In very poor families the children are fed at breakfast and supper chiefly upon bread, bread and treacle, or bread and butter, with so-called tea; whilst at dinner they have the same food, or boiled potato or cabbage smeared over it with a little fat from the bacon with which it was boiled, or in which it was fried.

E *Wives often ate less well than their husbands. Dr Edward Smith described one woman's diet in 1864:*

On Sundays she generally obtains a moderately good dinner, but on other days the food consists mainly of bread with a little butter or dripping, a plain pudding, and vegetables for dinner or supper, and weak tea.

Food was not always pure and fresh. Many shop-keepers added items to the food to make it look better. Leaves from sycamore trees were put into tea, milk was watered down and some children's sweets had poison put in them. There were at least eight factories in London in the 1840s which dried old tea leaves for re-sale.

F *The price of food in 1836:*

Flour 3 kg	4p
Oatmeal (like porridge) 2 kg	2p
Potatoes 2½ kg	1p
Meat 1 kg	about 5p
Bacon 1 kg	5p
Butter 1 kg	5p
Sugar 1 kg	about 2½p
Soap	about 2½p
Milk 1 litre	2p
Tea 1 kg	60p
Coffee 1 kg	20p

G *In 1857 in Manchester an investigation showed that a third of most food eaten had been spoilt:*

Rice and other cheap materials are mixed in sugar, and sold at full . . . price . . . cocoa . . . with fine brown earth . . . **strychnine** in beer, copper in pickles and bottled fruit, lead in mustard, iron in tea and chocolate.

H *A cartoon from* Punch, *1855:*

THE USE OF ADULTERATION.

Little Girl. "IF YOU PLEASE, SIR, MOTHER SAYS, WILL YOU LET HER HAVE A QUARTER OF A POUND OF YOUR BEST TEA TO KILL THE RATS WITH, AND A OUNCE OF CHOCOLATE AS WOULD GET RID OF THE BLACK BEADLES?"

Questions

1   Read source B.
a) What work was done by women in the home?
b) How might these women feel after a long day's work in the factory?
c) Do you think these women would be for or against factory reform? Give reasons.
d) Why do you think 55 per cent of women were against the Ten Hour Act?

2   Read sources C, D and E.
a) What is missing from these diets?
b) Why are the diets unhealthy?

3   Read source G.
a) What would the effects be of adulterating food?
b) How could stale meat be disguised?
c) Most working-class people shopped by gas-light on Friday and Saturday evenings. How easy would it be to disguise bad food? Explain your answer.

4   Look at source H.
a) What is being added to the food by the shopkeeper?
b) What could the sand be added to?
c) How reliable do you think this source is as evidence? Give reasons.

5   Read source F. Work out a weekly food bill for a family that earned between them £2.20 a week and paid 25p rent.

6   Look at source A. Compare wash-day in the past to wash-day in Britain today. Think about obtaining the water, heating it, soap, washing and drying, amongst others.

20 Looking after the Children

As most of the family went out to work, there were often no adults left to look after the infants. Young daughters often looked after the house and children during the day. Sometimes families hired a young girl from another family. This child might have to look after two or three babies.

A *Fourth Report of Medical Officer of the Privy Council, 1862:*

> Young girls, aged seven or eight years, are frequently removed from school for the purpose of taking charge of young children while the mother is absent at work.

Many parents used child-minders to look after their infants. Mothers carried their babies to the child-minder on their way to the mill at 5am and collected them at night. Sometimes mothers employed a child-minder who lived near the factory so that she could feed the baby at lunch-time.

B Morning Chronicle, *about 1850:*

> She carried her own child every morning to the nurse, rising for this purpose a full hour before she went to the mill, because the nurse lived some way off ... She did not **suckle** it in the course of the day, because the distances were too far to go.

If a mother could not breast-feed her baby she sometimes used a **wet-nurse**. Most working mothers could not afford their own wet-nurses. Working-class children often shared the milk with others.

C *In Ashton-under-Lyne one wet-nurse (1844) said that she:*

> ... nursed and suckled as many as three children at a time, that she had frequently been so exhausted by it as to be unable to walk across the room.

There was no powdered milk at this time so if a baby was not breast-fed it was bottle-fed on cows' milk. Old ginger beer bottles were often used as babies' bottles. These bottles were rarely washed properly. Rags were used instead of teats.

Artificial feeding can be very harmful. The World Health Organization today is against artificial feeding in the Third World because most people cannot **sterilise** the baby's bottle and it quickly becomes infected. In Victorian England, as in many poorer countries today, badly washed bottles were a main reason for small babies dying.

D *Fourth Report of the Medical Officer, 1862:*

> Pap made of bread and water sweetened with sugar and treacle is the sort of nourishment given during the mother's absence, even to infants of a very tender age, and in several instances little children, not more than six or seven years of age, were seen preparing and feeding the babies with this food.

Children were often in pain because they were so badly fed. This made it difficult for most nurses to look after them. To stop the babies crying many child-minders gave them syrup.

E *Evidence to* Select Committee on the Best Means of Protecting Infants put out to Nurse, *1871:*

> [The infants] are in constant pain and difficult to nurse; then they give them **cordial**; then they sleep a certain time. When they [wake] up again they feed

them, and then they cry, and then they give them some more cordial and this goes on all day.

All of these soothing syrups contained a strong drug such as opium, morphia or laudanum. Aniseed, treacle, sugar and laudanum were mixed together at home to make a sleeping drug. Infants of just a few months old were given the equivalent of two grains of opium. One soothing syrup called 'Godfreys' was a very popular drug.

F Morning Chronicle, *about 1850:*

Every druggist makes his own Godfrey, and the stronger he makes it the faster it is bought. The medicine consists of laudanum sweetened by a syrup, and further flavoured by some essential oil of spice.

Weaning infants at this time was a difficult task. Baby food was not available until 1867 and even then was much too expensive for most working people.

G *Dr Edward Smith, 1860:*

The infant is fed both before and after it is weaned upon a soup made with crumbs of bread, warm water and sugar, and in some cases a little milk is added. Bits of bread and butter, old meat, or any other kind of food which the mother may have in her hand are added, and not infrequently drops of gin and Godfreys cordial.

By the time the baby was one year old it was fed on whatever its parents ate – cheese, onions and even beer.

Over fifty per cent of working-class children in Manchester died before the age of five.

In December 1850, the first day-nursery in Lancashire was opened in Ancoats Crescent, Manchester. It opened from between 5.30 am and 7 pm every working day for children aged between one month and three years. The nursery charged 25p a week. This nursery soon closed down because of lack of money.

It was to be many years before nurseries were built by the government for the children of working parents.

Questions

1 a) What methods were used by working mothers to feed their babies?
   b) What were the advantages and disadvantages of each method?

2 Why was it so difficult for parents to sterilise babies' bottles?

3 a) Why did child-minders give young babies drugs?
   b) From the evidence, do you think the child-minders were aware of the dangers?

4 Do you think the nursery at Ancoats was used by many parents? Give reasons for your answer.

21 Entertainment

Most people worked very long hours. Sunday was their only day of rest. Some people took 'St Monday' off as well. Factory workers did not have a yearly holiday. Not until 1847 were workers given Saturday afternoon off.

In what little spare time they had, many people went to the pub. Pubs were open before six o'clock in the morning and did not close until after midnight. There was no age limit for drinking.

Many pubs had bowling, drama or skittle clubs. Some were used as job centres and to pay wages. Union meetings were also held in pubs. In many northern towns pubs had their own lending libraries. Lectures and meetings sometimes took place in the evening.

A *Edwin Rice, early nineteenth century:*

> Here a man can do nothing at a public house, if he goes there, but drink, and he can go nowhere else on a Sunday.

B *Samuel Bamford said this about factory workers in 1844:*

> . . . they are the greatest readers; can show the greatest number of good writers; the greatest . . . public speakers . . . the greatest number of poets and a greater number of musicians.

Some sport was more violent. People from all different backgrounds went to cock fighting and bear baiting. Cock fighting was still legal until 1849. Bears were sometimes buried up to their stomach in sand and attacked by dogs. In Lancashire a popular sport was 'purring'. Two men with clogs on their feet kicked each other until one gave in or was knocked out.

C *Memories of Bygone Manchester by Richard Wright Procter:*

> In those days, I remember the 12th Earl of Derby was a great support of cock fighting. During Whit week he used to stay at the Albion Hotel, Piccadilly, and about 12 o'clock each day [drove] down Market St in a carriage drawn by four horses to the cockpit.

Circuses were very popular. Liotard, the original 'Daring Young Man on the Flying Trapeze' was well known. A female human cannonball called Zazel also drew large crowds.

D *A circus advert, 1822:*

Before the age of the train only richer people could afford to travel far. Cheap rail tickets gave many more people the opportunity to leave the dirty, smoky cities for a day by the seaside. Blackpool became a popular seaside town.

Some factory owners took their workers on day trips. In 1836 a factory owner called Mr Barnes took 300 employees to Liverpool for the day. A special train left at 6 am to take his workers on an outing costing 20p each.

E *A railway advert from the 1840s:*

LANCASHIRE & YORKSHIRE
RAILWAY.

SEA BATHING
FOR THE
WORKING CLASSES,

ON AND AFTER SUNDAY MORNING NEXT,
and on each succeeding Sunday until further notice, with a view of affording the benefit of

SEA BATHING,

A Train will leave the following Stations for
FLEETWOOD AND BLACKPOOL.

FARES
THERE AND BACK THE SAME DAY.

		A.M.	Males.	Females & Children.
Leave Manchester at		6 0	3s. 0d.	1s. 6d.
„ Bolton at		6 30	2s. 6d.	1s. 3d.
„ Chorley at		7 10	2s. 0d.	1s. 0d.
„ Preston at		7 40	2s. 0d.	1s. 0d.

Arriving at Fleetwood at 9 a.m.

FROM SALFORD STATION.

MANCHESTER TO LIVERPOOL

FARES there and back same day.

	Males.	Females and Children.
At 7 a.m.	2s. 6d.	1s. 6d.

BURY TO LIVERPOOL, BLACKPOOL,
AND FLEETWOOD.

FARES there and back same day.

	Males.	Females and Children.
At 6 20 a.m.	2s. 6d.	1s. 6d.

Parties availing themselves of these trains will be enabled to

BATHE & REFRESH THEMSELVES

In ample time to attend a Place of Worship.

These Trains will return punctually at 6 p.m., arriving at Manchester about 8 and 9 p.m.

The Tickets will take the Passengers to the above-named places for ONE FARE, but for the purpose of preventing any unnecessary confusion or BUSINESS ON THE SUNDAY, it is desirable that tickets be taken on SATURDAY EVENING.

Bradshaw and Blacklock, Printers, 47, Brown-street, Manchester.

Questions

1 a) Read sources A and B. What do these sources tell us about leisure time?
b) How do these sources compare with the secondary text?
c) Which do you believe and why?

2 a) Would cock fighting have continued after 1849?
b) Some people think bull fighting, fox hunting and boxing are cruel sports today. How similar are they to sports in the past?

3 Look at source E.
a) Where did the Manchester trains go to?
b) What was the train fare for men, women and children?
c) Why do you think men were charged more than women?

4 Look at source D.
a) What acts could people see in this circus?
b) Circus owners encouraged people to come to the circus by putting up posters like these around the town. How else could people be encouraged to visit the circus?

22 Child Workers Today

It is the law in Britain today that every child up to the age of 16 must go to school. If pupils miss school for no reason their parents or **guardians** can be taken to court.

British children no longer have to go out to work to help to buy food for the family or to pay the rent. Children are not allowed to work full-time until they are 16. Teenagers sometimes work part-time to earn money to buy tapes, records or the latest fashions.

But in some parts of the world children do not go to school. They are expected to work full-time. They work long hours for very little pay. They have little choice. If they did not work they would not get enough to eat.

Many of these children are badly treated at work. Their conditions are very similar to those in the worst type of factory in the nineteenth century.

A *Young boys were paid 25p a week to make carpets which were later sold in Harrods for about £1200. Many of the children were employed by British companies.*

B Third World Now Magazine, *1983:*

Earlier in the year 27 children had been rescued from village carpet sheds, again in Mirzapur ... The boys, aged between six and ten were made to work twenty hours a day and were given one roti (bread) and watery lentils for their two daily meals.

They were woken at 4am by having water poured on them and then squatted at the looms until 2pm when they had a 'lunch' break of half an hour. They were forced to work again until midnight or later before having their second meal and being locked in one small room until restarting work the next day.

They received no pay, were confined to the work place and were frequently beaten with iron rods or wooden sticks or deliberately wounded with the scissors they used during the making of the carpets.

If they made a weaving mistake, asked for extra food or went to the lavatory without permission they were punished. If they cried, they were hit with stones tied in a piece of cloth.

Many of them became ill. On one occasion when several of them tried unsuccessfully to run away, they were punished by being slung upside down from a tree and branded, some of them in the arm pit.

C *In Morocco children do not have to go to school. Many families send their young children to work in the carpet factories. These families are very poor and the child's wage is needed. From an* Anti-Slavery Society *article:*

'With Morocco's carpet industry booming and fortunes being made rapidly by the factory owners, child workers have an important place ... In 28 factories/workshops at least one-third of the employees were under 12 ... These children were often only 8, 9 or 10 years old.

Hours were long: ... Wages were meagre, with so-called apprentices earning nothing. An annual holiday with pay – laid down by the law – was almost totally unknown.

In many of the factories visited the children looked undernourished and over-worked. While most factories and workshops had lavatories and running water, working conditions were often poor.

... a few of the small rug-making workshops ...

offered pleasant surroundings and a more friendly atmosphere than the larger factories where several hundred girls would be under the strict control of older women or male overseers.

... In general, a rug-making loom is worked by a team of four to eight girls. ... It is not uncommon in smaller workshops to find a loom being worked by only one or two girls ... The workers stand or sit on a bench, ... knotting with one hand and cutting off the wool with a pair of scissors or a knife with the other.'

D *Anti-slavery leaflet, 1986:*

'Why in the world do we need an anti-slavery society today?' Abuse of child labour is thought of as a nineteenth century evil that has been [got rid of]. The reality is that the labour of millions of children is still abused, often in conditions as horrific as in the factories of 150 years ago ...

In Thailand, India, Brazil, Morocco, Italy, South Africa and in many other countries ... adults see children only as a source of cheap and obedient labour.

If you think that it is only children in other countries who are badly treated, you are wrong. Although it is against British law to employ young children, not everyone obeys it. In August 1987, the 'Observer' newspaper reported that more than a million children worked illegally in the school holidays. One job was offered to a twelve year old at £15 for a forty five hour week. Part of this child's work was to pick pieces of cotton up off the floor. Other cases include a fourteen year old who worked on a loom in Tottenham and a young boy of the same age who use dangerous machinery in Norfolk. Some children were paid as little as 2p an hour.

It is also against the law to be cruel to children. Yet children have still been badly beaten and sometimes deliberately starved. Jasmine Beckford died from cruelty and neglect. Babies have been kept in cots and never spoken to or cuddled. Reports now show that children can also be the victims of sexual abuse.

So when we look back at life over a hundred years ago and think how lucky we are today, we must remember that people in the future might view our world quite differently.

Questions

1 Look at source A and read source C.
a) What are the young children doing?
b) Is source A likely to be a small or large workshop? Give reasons.

2 Look back to Chapter 6 on pages 14–15. Compare the life of Robert Blincoe with a young worker today. Mention work, hours, wages and conditions.

3 Look at source D.
a) What is the Anti-Slavery Society?
b) Why does it exist today?
c) The Anti-Slavery Society was founded in 1839. Can you think why?

4 Look back to Chapter 12 on pages 26–7.
a) What laws were passed to protect children?
b) Would similar laws work today? Give reasons for your answer.

5 Read source C.
a) Why did the Anti-Slavery Society write this article?
b) How reliable would this article be?

6 a) Why do you think some employers use young children as workers?
b) How could you make sure that employers obeyed the law?
c) How could you help children know their rights?

Glossary

artificial – made by people
autobiography – the story of one's own life
bonded – as a slave
cesspool – a pool of filthy water
civil war – war between people in the same country
commuter – someone who travels a long way to work
cordial – sweet drink
defendants – those on trial
diarrhoea – looseness of the bowels
draper's shop – shop selling material, cotton, needles etc
excreta – human body waste
genteel – ladylike
graduate – student
guardian – adult responsible for a child
hovel – very poor housing
labo(u)r – work
mitigation – lessening
overseer – man in charge of factory workers

patent rights – the right to sell or use an invention
piece-rates – paid by the amount produced
plantations – cotton farms
recreation – play
stagnant – dirty, smelly
sterilise – kill all the germs
strychnine – poison
suburban – living area on the edge of a town
suckle – breast-feed
tenters – someone who stretches the cloth
throstle spinner – someone who works a simple spinning machine
Tory – Conservative
universal – used all over the world
weaning – giving food instead of milk
wet-nurse – woman employed to breast-feed another woman's baby
workhouse – place where people without money could stay

Index

The Past in Question
Series Editor: J.F. Aylett

Life in the Industrial Revolution

Paula Bartley

Hodder & Stoughton

LONDON SYDNEY AUCKLAND TORONTO

Acknowledgements

The publishers would like to thank the following for their permission to reproduce copyright illustrations. Longman & Co/Hansard, p4. The British Library Newspaper Library, p5. The John Rylands University Library, Manchester, p6. BBC Hulton Picture Library, pp7 top, 32, cover. Chris Aspin, pp7 bottom, 16. The Mansell Collection Ltd, pp8, 12 bottom, 15, 20 top left, 21 top, 27 left & right, 30, 37 (Punch) & 41 (Punch). The Illustrated London News, p9 photographed from *A New Historical and Descriptive View of Derbyshire* by D P Davies, p12 top. The Documentary Photography Archive Manchester Polytechnic, pp13, 14, 17 photographed from *A Memoir of Robert Blincoe* by John Brown. New Lanark Conservation, pp18 left & right & 19. Manchester Central Library, Local History Department, pp20 bottom left & 44 photographed from *The White Slaves of England* by John Cobden, p20 right. City of Manchester Art Gallery, p21 bottom. University of London Library/Harpers Monthly vol 8, p23 left & right. The Victoria and Albert Museum, p24. Peter Newark's Western Americana and Historical Pictures, p25 left & right. British Museum, p31. Neville Cooper, p33. Guildhall Library, City of London, pp34 & 38. B T Batsford Ltd, pp36 (Liverpool Corporation) & 45 (Manchester Public Libraries). Tyne & Wear Museums Service/Sunderland Museum & Art Galleries, p39 top. The Museum of London, p39 bottom. Topham Picture Library, p40. The Anti Slavery Society, p46.

I would like to thank all those who have helped in the publication of this book, especially Hilary Bourdillon, Noeline Crow and Vicky Robinson. Special thanks to John Aylett for his support.

British Library Cataloguing in Publication Data

Bartley, Paula
   Life in the Industrial Revolution.—
   (The Past in question).
   1. Industrialization—Social aspects
   I. Title   II. Series
   303.4′83′091812 HD82

   ISBN 0 7131 7650 4

First published 1987
Third impression 1989

Printed in Great Britain for the educational publishing division of Hodder and Stoughton Ltd, Mill Road, Dunton Green, Sevenoaks, Kent by St Edmundsbury Press Ltd, Bury St Edmunds, Suffolk.